Ocean Animals

Dolphins

by Christina Leaf

BELLWETHER MEDIA
MINNEAPOLIS, MN

Blastoff! Beginners are developed by literacy experts and educators to meet the needs of early readers. These engaging informational texts support young children as they begin reading about their world. Through simple language and high frequency words paired with crisp, colorful photos, Blastoff! Beginners launch young readers into the universe of independent reading.

Blastoff! Universe

Reading Level

BLASTOFF! Beginners — Grade K

BLASTOFF! READERS — Grades 1-3

BLASTOFF! DISCOVERY — Grade 4

Sight Words in This Book 🔍

a	for	look	the	to
and	have	make	their	use
are	in	many	there	water
be	is	of	these	
big	it	on	they	
can	like	play	this	

This edition first published in 2021 by Bellwether Media, Inc.

No part of this publication may be reproduced in whole or in part without written permission of the publisher. For information regarding permission, write to Bellwether Media, Inc., Attention: Permissions Department, 6012 Blue Circle Drive, Minnetonka, MN 55343.

Library of Congress Cataloging-in-Publication Data

Names: Leaf, Christina, author.
Title: Dolphins / by Christina Leaf.
Description: Minneapolis, MN : Bellwether Media, 2021. | Series: Blastoff! beginners : Ocean animals | Includes bibliographical references and index. | Audience: Grades PreK-2
Identifiers: LCCN 2020008618 (print) | LCCN 2020008619 (ebook) | ISBN 9781644873243 (library binding) | ISBN 9781681038117 (paperback) | ISBN 9781681037875 (ebook)
Subjects: LCSH: Marine animals--Juvenile literature.
Classification: LCC QL122.2 .L43 2021 (print) | LCC QL122.2 (ebook) | DDC 591.77--dc23
LC record available at https://lccn.loc.gov/2020008618
LC ebook record available at https://lccn.loc.gov/2020008619

Editor: Amy McDonald   Designer: Andrea Schneider

Printed in the United States of America, North Mankato, MN.

Table of Contents

Dolphins! 4

Body Parts 10

Pods 16

Dolphin Facts 22

Glossary 23

To Learn More 24

Index 24

Dolphins!

Look in the water!
It is a dolphin!

Dolphins are fun ocean animals. They like to play!

There are many kinds of dolphins. Most are gray.

bottlenose

striped

Amazon river

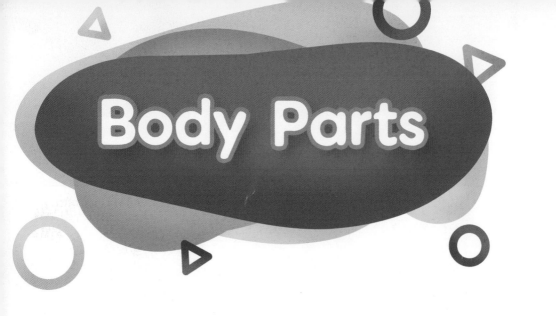

Body Parts

Dolphins have a **fin**. It is on their backs.

fin

Dolphins have **flippers** and a tail. They use these to swim.

tail

flippers

13

Dolphins have
a **blowhole**.
It takes in air.

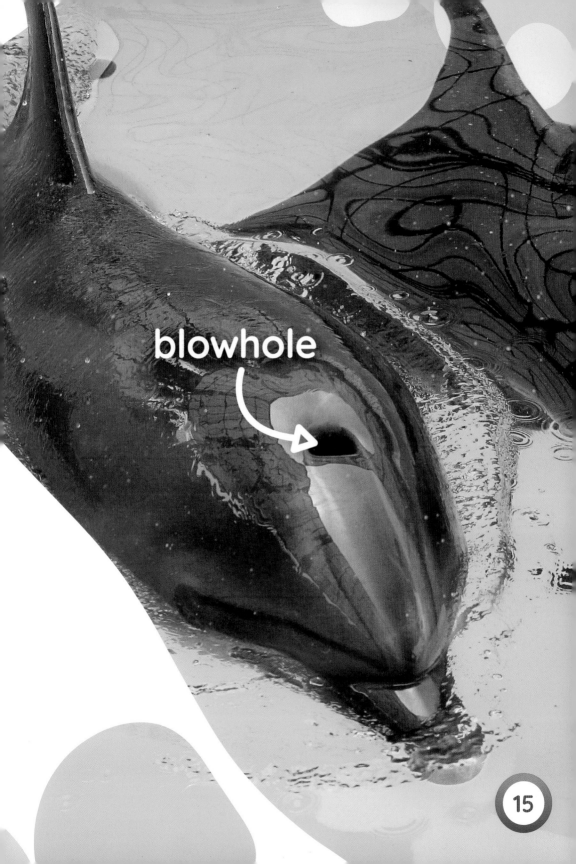

blowhole

15

Pods

Dolphins live
in **pods**.
These groups can
be big or small.

pod

This pod hunts
for fish.
It is a team.

Pods talk!
They make
a lot of noise.
Click! Squeak!

Dolphin Facts

Dolphin Body Parts

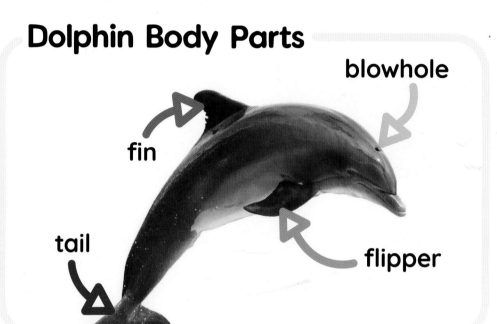

blowhole

fin

tail

flipper

Dolphin Food

fish   squids   shrimp

Glossary

blowhole

a hole that dolphins use to breathe

fin

a flat body part on the backs of dolphins

flippers

wide, flat body parts dolphins use to swim

pods

groups of dolphins

To Learn More

ON THE WEB

FACTSURFER

Factsurfer.com gives you a safe, fun way to find more information.

1. Go to www.factsurfer.com.

2. Enter "dolphins" into the search box and click 🔍.

3. Select your book cover to see a list of related content.

Index

air, 14

blowhole, 14, 15

fin, 10, 11

fish, 18

flippers, 12, 13

hunts, 18

kinds, 8

noise, 20

ocean, 6

play, 6

pods, 16, 17, 18, 20

swim, 12

tail, 12, 13

talk, 20

team, 18

water, 4

The images in this book are reproduced through the courtesy of: Andrea Izzotti, front cover, p. 23 (flippers); Potapov Alexander, p. 3; Willyam Bradberry, pp. 4-5, 6-7; michaelgeyer_photography, pp. 8-9; R. Maximiliane, p. 8 (bottlenose); Romain_brz, p. 9 (striped); Coulanges, p. 9 (Amazon river); WaterFrame/ Alamy Stock Photo, pp. 10-11; Shahar Shabtai, pp. 12-13; Elena Larina, pp. 14-15; imageBroker/ Alamy Stock Photo, pp. 16-17; Miroya Minakuchi/ Minden Pictures, pp. 18-19; Neirfy, p. 22 (parts); evantravels, p. 22 (fish); Lauren Squire, p. 22 (squids); MF Choi, p. 22 (shrimp); Sokolov Alexey, p. 23 (blowholes); Antonio Gravante, p. 23 (fin); F Photography R, p. 23 (pods).